Best Golf Tips of All Time

1,000 Nuggets to Noodle

Tom Metz

 Whimpering
Flagsticks
Press

Published by Whimpering Flagsticks Press,
an imprint of Bettencourt Publishing Ltd.,
Seattle, Washington.

For information about special discounts for
bulk purchases, please contact us through
the website: www.bettencourtpub.com.

Metz, Thomas V., 1951-
Best Golf Tips of All Time: 1,000 Nuggets to
Noodle / Thomas V. Metz, Jr.

ISBN: 978-0-9898398-1-5

Table of Contents

Introduction

What I like about golf is that the ball always goes exactly where I hit it. This book will help you like where you hit it more often.

Some people say you should have only one, or at most two, swing thoughts. Well, we will have none of that! As a contrarian, my philosophy is entirely different. I say the more the better. If one or two swing thoughts are good then 10 or 20 are really good, 50 are absolutely great and 1,000 are nothing short of fantastic! Yep, you can never have too many swing thoughts.

All this talk about keeping the mind clear is completely wrong. If we were all Zen masters we would be too at peace to go aggravate ourselves with a round of golf. Swing thoughts are wonderful! Swing thoughts are the essence of golf. Without swing thoughts there is nothing; golf would be nothing!

For us golfers, that little subconscious is a powerful thing. It can override the conscious almost every time. So we need to whip that subconscious into shape, tell it what to do. The best way to do that is to be armed with some swing thoughts...like perhaps 1,000 of them! Your subconscious will not stand a chance.

Many of these swing thoughts may not resonate with you; but a few of them will. There even may be an "aha!" moment. Everybody is different. A swing thought that works for one person may not be helpful to another person. That is the beauty of golf; it is so individual. Peruse the list of thoughts and see which ones work for you. Of 1,000 swing thoughts there are probably a few that you will find helpful.

The book started out as a joke among my golf friends. They would tease me, saying that I had so many swing thoughts that I needed a database to keep track of them all. Being an analytical sort, this seemed quite natural to me. I don't know what their problem is. Anyway, I ended up with a lot of swing thoughts. So here they are.

You may notice that a number of these golf tips are repeated in the book. This is intentional. Some golf tips are too important not to mention them multiple times. For example, keeping the right knee bent on the takeaway. The intent is to drive home the key concepts that are critical to the golf swing.

Reviewing a handful of swing thoughts every day is a pleasant and fruitful exercise. Who doesn't enjoy thinking about golf? Sometimes I lie in bed before falling asleep and my mind trundles over to golf. I visualize my swing. It is constructive and relaxing to review a few swing thoughts before drifting off.

Visualization can improve athletic performance in any sport, but particularly in golf. Read five or 10 tips a day and contemplate them. Create a picture in your mind. Imagine yourself doing the swing just like the tip says.

Picture your body moving that way.

When you wonder why the ball went where it did instead of where you wanted it to go, what should you do? Well, that's when you reach for this book and discover a passel of swing thoughts to solve your problem. No golf bag is complete without this book; no nightstand is complete without this book. One can never have too many swing thoughts.

Count of swing thoughts

Chipping	77
Pitching	53
Putting	113
Sand Shots	92
Full Swing	629
Practice	36
Total:	1,000

Chipping

Pick a spot to land every chip.

———————————————————

Take three practice swings on chips.

———————————————————

Don't scoop the ball when chipping.

———————————————————

Put three-quarters of your weight on your left leg.

———————————————————

Make a sharp, descending strike on the ball.

———————————————————

Change the ball position to control
how far the ball will go.

Pretend your hands are dead when
you chip.

Follow through with a low finish.

Play the ball off your right heel.

Use your sand wedge for most chips.

Alter the length of the back swing to
control distance.

Keep the heel of the club off the ground
when chipping from the fringe.

Let your wrists hinge naturally.

Keep your lower body quiet.

With a lob wedge, hinge your wrists quickly on the back swing.

Follow through, turning your chest to the target.

Don't let the club pass your hands.

For backspin, focus on hitting down on the ball, not behind it.

Pinch the ball against the turf.

Use a lower lofted club if you have more green to work with.

Loosen your grip pressure on chips.

Don't cock your wrists.

You must strike down on the ball, not scoop under it.

Make sure you hit the ball first, not the ground.

Use your putting grip for short chips.

Do not decelerate on chips.

Don't try to lift the ball off the ground.

Make a rhythmical swing, not jerky.

Let the club do the work.

Be sure to accelerate through with the lob wedge.

Don't force a lob wedge; let the club weight control the speed.

Keep arms and wrists passive on chips.

––––––––––––––––––

Turn through faster or slower to determine distance.

––––––––––––––––––

Relax and commit to the shot.

––––––––––––––––––

From a few feet off the green, lift the heel of the club and swing like you are putting.

––––––––––––––––––

Set up for chips with your hands well ahead of the ball.

––––––––––––––––––

Play the ball way back in your stance.

––––––––––––––––––

Use your right arm to control your chip shots.

If you are several feet off the green, chip with a 7 or 8 iron.

On chips, the left wrist should stay flat at impact.

When chipping from the fringe, strike down on the ball.

Always accelerate on chips.

Use a more lofted club for a short chip.

On long chips, use a club with less loft.

Keep your hands ahead of the club head at impact.

Move your chest and arms in unison.

Use a slightly weaker grip on chips.

Chip with a short back swing and a longer follow-through.

Choke down 2 or 3 inches for more control on chips.

The body should turn forward along with the arms.

Don't try to help the ball into the air;
let the club do it.

Chip with a 9 iron when two feet off
the green.

On chips, make sure your hands are
head of the ball at impact.

Do not use your wrists when chipping.

The length of your swing is
determined by the length of the shot.

On short downhill chips, abbreviate
your follow through.

Use a smooth tempo for all chips.

On hardpan, set up with the heel of
the club off the ground.

Don't try to lift the ball up.

When putting from off the green with
a 3 wood, choke down on the shaft.

In deep rough, hit behind the ball,
just like you would in sand.

On short chips, use the same motion
as your putting stroke.

Keep the left wrist firm through
impact on chips.

Try chipping with the same grip as
your putter grip.

Chip with your chin high and your
back straight.

Restrict your follow-through for
shorter chips.

Look at the front part of the ball
when chipping.

Play the ball back in your stance
when chipping from hardpan.

Stick your butt out on chips and putts.

Move your arms and shoulders as one unit.

When hitting from the rough around the green, commit to the shot.

When chipping, take a short backswing and accelerate.

Concentrate on making good contact with the ball.

When chipping with a low iron, choke down on the club.

Try to keep your wrists quiet.

Do not take a long backswing for a chip.

Use a more lofted club from the rough around the green.

Ramblings: Number 1 Mistake— Straightening the Right Knee

Straightening the right knee when taking the club back is the biggest mistake that amateurs make. The result is the transfer of your weight to the left side on the backswing. This is a reverse pivot. If your weight is already on your left side on the backswing, it is impossible to transfer the weight to your left leg when swinging down. There is no weight transfer and power is lost. I have several friends who golf this way and they hit weak drives. It is a difficult habit to change.

The fix is simple; just keep your right knee bent as you take the club back. Keep it bent the whole time. It is more athletic to swing when your right knee is bent than when your right knee is straight.

Swinging a club in slow motion is a good way to develop this habit. Now back to the swing thoughts.

Pitching

Place the ball just forward of center with respect to your heels.

Keep the clubface open through impact.

Accelerate through as you swing.

When using a lob wedge, play the ball slightly forward in your stance.

Use a little wider stance with a lob wedge.

Your body should rotate around your left hip.

Approach the ball from the inside.

Grip down one inch on the club.

Quiet the lower body.

Keep your swing tempo the same for each shot.

Pinch the ball against the turf with short irons and wedge shots.

Don't quit on the shot.

Hit the ball with a descending blow.

Keep turning through the shot; don't
stop.

With the lob wedge, think about sliding
the club just under the ball.

Close the clubface for a low, running
shot.

On a short pitch, keep your stance
narrow.

Keep your weight forward with the lob wedge.

With a lob wedge, open the face and then lower the hands.

Maintain the wrist hinge on the downswing on short pitches.

Use an extra club or two when pitching to an elevated green.

Use a consistent tempo on all chips and pitches.

With a lob wedge, think about driving your right arm under the ball.

When hitting from tall grass, don't turn your right forearm over your left forearm.

For a half wedge shot, place the ball in the middle of your stance.

Be sure to turn your hips as you swing.

On a downhill shot, chase the ball down the slope.

For shorter distances, choke down and take a normal swing.

Keep your hands ahead of the ball at impact.

Use a slightly weaker grip with a lob wedge.

Focus on making good contact with the ball.

On short pitches, swing from 9 o'clock to 3 o'clock.

Put more weight on your left side for a shot from 40 to 60 yards.

With a lob wedge, keep the clubface pointing up after impact.

You are better off pitching from 100 yards than 50 yards; the ball will spin and stop.

———————————

Keep your head very still for shots with a lob wedge.

———————————

When pitching, open the clubface to make the ball fly higher and land softer.

———————————

For a shorter pitch, take the club back only to the 9 o'clock position.

———————————

Don't uncock your wrists too early on pitches.

———————————

To hit a high pitch shot, lower your hands at address.

Play the ball off the toe of your lob wedge.

When hitting a pitch, set up by letting your arms hang down naturally.

Turn your shoulders and arms together for a pitch.

Rotate your chest through and toward the target on pitches.

Use your sand wedge for pitch shots closer than 80 yards.

When hitting a pitch shot, you should pinch the ball against the ground.

26

Remember to hit down on the ball on pitch shots.

For a flop shot take a long slow full swing.

Your stance should be slightly open with your 9 iron and wedges.

Relax and swing smoothly.

For a short wedge shot, keep your weight on your left leg.

For a lob wedge shot, swing a little outside-in.

Use a three-quarter backswing for a
65 yard shot.

Putting

The faster the green, the more break there will be.

Wet grass does not break as much.

Aim for an intermediate target, a foot in front of the ball.

Accelerate slightly through impact.

Let your arms hang easily under your shoulders.

Focus on controlling the speed of the putt.

On downhill putts, think about hitting the ball 50% or 70% of normal speed.

Be sure to accelerate on short putts.

Widen your stance when putting in wind.

Try giving more break than you normally would to avoid missing on the low side.

The putter should release just like an iron shot.

Keep your elbows in close on putts.

Never rush the stroke.

Let gravity help you with your putt.

Keep the putter low after impact.

On really long putts, take a longer backswing; do not swing faster.

Keep your head down on putts.

When putting put slightly more weight on your left leg.

Exhale during the forward stroke.

On long putts, accelerate smoothly.

Err on the higher side of the hole
when reading the break.

Your eyes should be one inch inside
the target line.

Don't jab at the ball.

Swing back on a low, level path.

Hit up slightly on the ball to get it rolling nicely.

Keep your head still.

A missed putt should go at least a foot past the cup.

On side-hill putts, break the shot down into two parts and then hit the first part.

Don't push the putter head through the ball.

Align your shoulders and feet parallel to the target line.

Swing from low to high.

Develop a rhythm for your putts...back and through.

Aim for the highest point of the break.

When putting, move your arms and shoulders together.

Begin reading the green as you are walking towards the green.

Open your stance a little on long putts.

When in doubt, always play for more break.

———————————————

Let the club follow through and release.

———————————————

Breathe a long breath before the putt.

———————————————

Keep your arms and chest in synch as you swing.

———————————————

Keep your hands ahead of the ball as you swing the putter.

———————————————

Think...the ball wants to go in the hole.

———————————————

Walk up to the hole to feel the green with your feet on every putt.

Don't let your hands get involved in the putt.

Use the same routine for every putt.

Don't break your wrists during the putt.

Relax your shoulders.

Don't move your head during your putt.

Swing slower on downhill putts.

A putt will often break toward the water.

Speed is more important than direction.

The ball is not moving, the hole is not moving; how hard could this be?

Always try to have consistent speed on your putts.

Watch the ball roll past the hole to read the break for the next putt.

Ramblings: Number 2 Mistake— Swinging with your Arms

When I watch people at the driving range, about 90% of them make their golf swings primarily with their arms. This is natural because we use our arms for many of our activities—such as hammering a nail, sawing a board, painting the house, washing the car; you get the idea. It is not a natural thing to swing a golf club with your upper body and arms moving together. It is a learned thing.

But it is not hard to learn. Simply practice swinging your arms and chest together. There is a drill that you may have seen that involves holding the golf club with the handle against your chest and your arms straight out. Then you turn back and through moving your arms and chest together. It takes some practice but is not a difficult thing.

Always read putts from below the hole,
not above the hole.

Don't look up until the ball has gone
six feet from you.

Relax after setting up.

The slower the ball rolls the more the
break will affect it.

Hit short putts firmly to take away
the break.

Don't ever be afraid to putt. You love
to putt.

Be sure to accelerate through the ball on uphill putts.

Study the last five feet of the putt because that is where it will break the most.

The speed of the putt determines how much it will break.

Vary the length of the backswing to get the right distance.

On long putts, aim for a three-foot circle around the hole.

Swing by turning your shoulders around your spine.

Let your arms hang down naturally.

Concentrate on speed more than the line of the putt.

Roll your putts; don't push through them.

Don't hunch over.

Don't flick your wrists on putts.

Rhythm and tempo are critical on putts.

On a long putt, pick a spot four feet away and aim there.

Rock your arms and shoulders as one unit.

Think about how far back to take the putter.

Make sure your feet are square to the target line.

Your wrists should not bend during the putting stroke.

Use a nice even tempo as you swing back and through.

Do not jab at the ball.

Bend at the hips.

On long putts, do not swing fast or rush it.

Follow through beyond your left hip.

On downhill putts, use lighter grip pressure.

Don't take too big of a back swing with the putter.

Keep your left wrist firm throughout the stroke.

Pretend you are confident, even if you are not.

Swing smoothly back and through on long putts.

Take just one practice swing.

Try using a shorter backswing to increase accuracy.

Press your hands forward when
setting up to putt.

———————————————

When putting, let the shoulders and
arms do most of the work.

———————————————

Accelerate through impact on every
putt.

———————————————

A shorter putting stroke is usually
better.

———————————————

Divide a double breaking putt into
several sections.

———————————————

For an uphill putt, pretend the hole is
farther away.

———————————————

Stand up taller for long putts.

For very long putts, use a slight wrist cock.

Choke down on the grip when putting on a fast green.

Hitting the putt on the toe of the club will deaden the putt.

Take a short backswing on putts and follow through.

Stick your butt out a little when setting up for a putt.

For putts 15 feet and shorter, your ball should always go past the hole unless it drops in.

Be relaxed and set up comfortably for every putt.

For downhill putts, pretend the hole is closer than it really is.

Remember that downhill putts will break more than uphill putts.

For a downhill putt, swing a little slower.

Putt by simply rocking your shoulders.

Let the putter swing freely.

Take the putter back low to the ground.

Focus on a spot on the ball before you swing the putter.

Think more about how hard to hit the ball than the perfect line.

Never, ever decelerate on a putt.

The ball position should be a little bit forward.

Sand Shots

Play the ball forward in your stance
so the club strikes the sand first.

Hit one or two inches of sand behind
the ball.

Open the clubface and aim a little left.

Make a full finish with sand shots.

Put your weight on the inside of your
left foot.

Keep a firm left wrist through impact.

On a downhill lie, follow through down the slope.

Use a sand wedge, not a lob wedge, and open the face.

Rotate your hips and torso through the shot.

Shift your weight forward as you swing.

With only one foot in the sand, swing with your arms only.

Hinge your wrists fully on sand shots.

In the sand, play the ball farther forward, off your left heel.

On a buried lie, bend your knees more.

Set up with your hands low in a bunker.

From a long greenside bunker shot, make sure to release the club.

Follow through, follow through, follow through.

Accelerate your swing when in the sand.

In fairway bunkers, try sweeping the ball.

Rotate the clubface open to hit a shorter shot.

Rotate the clubface closed to get more distance.

Swing through and accelerate.

Open your stance a little and swing along your stance line.

A full swing sand wedge shot from a trap will go one-third as far if from grass.

In downhill sand, tilt your shoulders to match the slope.

To hit a high sand shot, swing through at a higher speed.

If the ball is above your feet, play it back in your stance.

In wet or hard sand, do not open the clubface; dig the leading edge under the ball.

For a high and short shot, open the clubface even more.

———————————————

Point the grip of the club just to the right of your belt buckle at set-up.

———————————————

Widen your stance in the sand.

———————————————

Turn your chest toward the target as you swing.

———————————————

With a thin lie in sand, use a pitching wedge to avoid bouncing the club off the sand.

———————————————

Follow through high to your left shoulder.

———————————————

Don't flip your wrists.

For a longer shot, follow through more.

At set-up, the club should be parallel to your left leg.

Select a spot to land the ball on the fly.

Swing with a shallow arc if the ball is above your feet.

Open your stance in wet sand.

Ramblings: Number 3 Mistake — Poor Tempo

When I watch a good golfer, I am always impressed by their great tempo. Some swing fairly slowly, some swing relatively fast and some are in the middle, but their tempo is always smooth. Back and through. There is no rush.

I have learned to take the club back more slowly because then I don't do bad things at the top. This has helped my tempo because prior to this adjustment I was swinging too fast.

Some golf pros tell students to pause briefly at the top and other pros do not think this is a good idea. It doesn't really matter as far as tempo is concerned. I like the phrase 'slow from the top' because it promotes good tempo. You can't learn tempo from a book so I have no intention of trying to describe how to do it. Just work on it.

The more you open the clubface, the more you should open your stance.

With a high lip, play the ball more forward in your stance.

The bottom of the club head should contact the sand first, not the leading edge.

Swing hard on sand shots, especially if there is a high lip.

Do not unhinge your wrists too early.

Accelerate on the downswing in sand.

Swing faster or slower for higher or lower ball flight.

Keep your feet apart when in sand.

You want a quiet lower body in sand.

Let the club release when on a down slope.

In the sand, the club head should pass your hands before it gets to the ball.

Use a pitching wedge or 9 iron for a longer bunker shot.

Stay aggressive on sand shots.

With a buried lie in sand, close the clubface.

On sand shots, hold the clubface open as you swing through.

In wet sand, keep the clubface more closed.

Always make a full follow-through from the sand.

On firm sand, keep your weight forward.

On bunker shots, make sure to keep the club moving through impact.

Use a weaker grip when hitting from sand.

Choke down a little when hitting from a bunker.

Keep your left knee bent slightly in the sand.

For a 40-yard bunker shot, use your 8 or 9 iron, not your sand wedge.

Your swing path should be from out to in when hitting from sand.

Put most of your weight on your left
leg when hitting from sand.

Control the distance of a sand shot by
how fast you turn your body through.

For a short bunker shot, open the
clubface and have a short follow
through.

Align your feet slightly left of your target
when hitting from a bunker.

Keep the clubface square for a long
bunker shot.

For a high bunker shot, open your feet 30° and open up the clubface.

Take a wide stance when hitting from a downhill lie in a bunker.

Choke down on the club with an uphill lie in a bunker.

Open the clubface and take a long shallow divot in the sand.

In the sand, the club head should get to the ball before your hands.

In wet sand, use a 60° lob wedge and choke down.

With a fried-egg lie, use a steep downswing and more wrist hinge.

Keep your head still when hitting from the sand.

Squat down a little when setting up for a sand shot.

Swing aggressively on most sand shots.

In the sand, take a wider stance with more knee flex.

In a deep bunker, use a more vertical backswing.

Do not uncock your wrists too early in the sand.

Use your pitching wedge when hitting from sand near the lip of the bunker.

The pace of your swing determines distance when hitting from a bunker.

With a downhill lie in a bunker, swing the club down the slope.

In a bunker, play the ball forward in your stance so you can easily hit behind it.

Choke down when hitting from a fairway bunker.

Take a three-quarter backswing when hitting from a fairway bunker.

With a plugged lie, swing down on a steeper path.

Keep your lower body more still when hitting sand shots.

Make sure you have enough club-head speed to get the ball to the hole.

Make a full turn for a long green-side bunker shot.

The Full Swing

Keep your right knee bent on the
backswing.

Make sure your head is behind the ball.

Let the club do the work.

Keep your chin up.

As you swing, force your left heel down.

The takeaway should be low and slow.

Keep your left arm straight.

Grip the club lightly.

Visualize the finish position.

Coil by turning your hips as far as they will turn and keep the right knee bent.

Start the downswing by moving the left knee to the left.

Pause at the top.

Put your left shoulder under your chin.

Hands loose and relaxed.

On the backswing, place your left shoulder over the right knee.

Do not sway to the right; coil instead.

Turn your shoulders on the takeaway, don't tilt them.

On upslope shots, position your shoulders level with the slope.

Keep your left arm close to chest.

Start the swing by letting the club drop.

Rotate the forearms, crossing them over as you swing.

Shift your weight and step into the ball.

Extend both arms just after impact.

Turn your right hip forward and up just as you hit the ball.

Keep your right elbow near your right side.

Put about 90% of your weight on your right foot at the top of your backswing.

On the downswing, transfer your weight to your left side.

Clear your hips out of the way so your arms can swing freely.

Swing using only 80% power with your driver.

Visualize a nice follow-through.

The left eye should be just back of the ball.

Swing the hands through on the path
you want the ball to travel.

The ball goes where the hands go.

Play the ball off the toe when hitting
the lob wedge.

Swing with relaxed arms and wrists.

Keep the club head in front of your
body on the takeaway.

Rotate your chest toward the target.

Use an abbreviated finish on a knockdown shot.

Accelerate the club through impact.

Allow your head to move a little as you swing.

When your body stops turning on the backswing, your arms should stop too.

Keep your hips turning level through the swing.

On upslope shots, swing along the surface of the slope.

Ramblings: Number 4 Mistake— Not Accelerating Past Impact

Accelerating the club is one of the most magical moves that we can do with any golf swing. It is critical to accelerate through the ball on every shot: drives, long irons, short irons, chips and putts. Swing slowly from the top and then gradually accelerate. This is an excellent way to hit a golf ball. Accelerating will also help your putting and chipping.

The club head should continue to accelerate after impact. This is not a hit; it is a swing. That is why this book is about "swing thoughts," not "hitting thoughts." The ball just happens to get in the way of your swing. Too many golfers think about it as a hit. You can see them at the practice range—hit, hit, hit.

Swinging, rather than hitting, is a different mental picture. Don't hit *at* the ball, swing *through* the ball. And the best way to hit through the ball is to continue accelerating the club past the ball. Give it a try; it actually works great.

Keep your arm swing synchronized with your body turn.

Start the swing with the left hip; bump it back and left.

Keep your head still.

Rotate your hips all the way through impact.

Aim at a spot five feet beyond the ball.

Let your hands release after you have struck the ball.

Start the downswing from the ground up.

Keep the club out, but the left arm in.

Your hips should end up over the left foot after the swing.

Think—"left shoulder...right shoulder."

On a tight lie, trap the ball between the club and the ground.

For a draw, place the ball back in your stance.

Choke down on shots within 120
yards to get correct distance.

Turn so your back faces the target.

The left hand should be leading at
impact.

Take a tall stance in a fairway
bunker.

In deep rough, hinge the wrists quickly
and swing down steeply.

Use the same swing for long irons as
you do for a wedge.

Set up with shoulders parallel to
target line.

Close your stance to hit a draw.

Turn your left foot out to allow more
hip turn.

Make a smooth weight shift.

Clear your left hip on the downswing.

Finish in a balanced position.

Stay loose and swing freely.

Drive the right shoulder down and through the ball.

At the top, the shaft should be parallel with the target line.

Tee the ball higher for a draw.

Don't try to swing too hard.

Follow through completely and in a flowing motion.

Don't make your hips too active on the downswing.

Continue rotating your right shoulder through until it points at the target.

Stay on plane on the backswing.

At the top, your shoulders should be behind the ball.

Don't have too much tension in your arms.

Too narrow a stance will restrict hip turn.

Make a full shoulder turn.

Don't let the club pass the hands at impact.

Maintain flex in the knee as your weight shifts right.

Don't start the downswing with your arms.

Pull the club back with your right shoulder.

For a draw, aim right and toe in the club.

Finish low for a penetrating shot into the wind.

Shift your weight to the right on the backswing.

To curve the ball right, aim your body to the left.

To curve the ball left, aim your body to the right.

Keep your head behind the ball through impact.

Tee the ball lower for a fade.

The toe of the club should pass the heel as it releases.

Do not cast the club by coming over the top.

If between clubs, choke down on the longer club and swing aggressively.

Keep the club moving through impact.

Don't bend over too far.

Place your weight on the balls of your feet, not your heels.

Think about your swing plane as you swing.

Keep hips level on the turn away;
don't tilt them.

Don't get your hands too close to
your body.

In wind, move the ball back in your
stance.

Finish with your right shoulder
under your chin.

Keep your lower body quiet on
fairway bunker shots.

Don't sway to the left as you swing.

Let your arms hang freely in front of you.

Don't dip past parallel at the top.

Maintain soft arms on the short irons.

Don't force the shot; let it go.

Flex your knees just before you swing back.

Move the ball back in your stance to make good contact with short irons.

As you turn through, keep your elbows close together.

Take the club back slowly; there is no hurry.

Keep your hands away from your head at the top.

Widen your stance in windy conditions.

Plant your feet solidly in fairway bunkers.

Stay calm at the top.

Extend your arms fully on the backswing.

Complete your backswing before
starting your downswing.

Concentrate on rhythm throughout
the swing.

Swing long irons the same way as
short irons.

The club head should continue to
accelerate after impact.

Try to achieve a free release of the
club head.

Keep your hands cocked as you
swing down.

As you start down, press on the ball
of your left foot.

Swing freely and with even tempo.

On long irons, keep your lower body
as still as possible.

Think "rhythm" just before taking the
club back.

End with your right shoulder over
your left leg.

Keep your butt out and your back
straight.

Relax your grip.

For a draw, fold your right arm over your left on the follow-through.

Tilt slightly to your right at set-up.

At set-up, bend your knees a little and bend from the hips.

Pull your shoulder blades together at the top.

Swing with an inside path to the ball.

Take one less club on a downhill lie.

Uncoil from the ground up.

Do not straighten the right knee on
the backswing.

When hitting from tall grass, aim more
right since the grass will grab the club
head.

When in doubt always take more club.

On the takeaway, keep the left arm in.

Start the downswing by bumping left
with your left hip.

Don't straighten up at the top.

Swing through, not down, with the
driver.

When hitting from a divot, position
the ball back in your stance.

Don't swing harder on long bunker
shots.

On a knockdown shot, make sure to
extend your arms through impact.

Ramblings: Number 5 Mistake—Putting with a Long Backswing

Taking too big a backswing is the number one putting mistake. It is better to take a short backswing and then swing forward with slight acceleration. The idea is to take as little backswing as possible.

One time I tried to teach a friend this trick by putting my foot right behind his putter. He could not swing back at all and it was interesting to see his reaction. He froze and could not putt. Finally, he got the idea. He swung the putter with minimal backswing.

This is a good way to develop a short backswing. Try putting with *no* backswing. And I mean no backswing, zip, zero, nil, not even an inch. This is particularly effective for short putts, about three or four feet. We usually accelerate on long putts but not on short putts. Give it a try.

Rotate your hips until they meet
resistance.

On a downwind shot, spin the ball
more than usual.

Visualize a fluid motion.

For a fade, hold off on releasing the
club.

Do not start the downswing with the
upper body.

Transfer your weight to the left and
unwind the hips.

Let your hands and arms drop
naturally.

Swing easier when into the wind.

Keep your shoulders and arms
connected on takeaway.

When hitting from a divot, use a
descending blow.

The left shoulder should turn down
and under your chin, to maintain
spine angle.

Hit with the right palm facing downward with fairway woods.

Set up for the driver with the ball opposite the left arm pit.

Your arms should hang directly under your shoulders.

Keep your right knee bent to prevent the hips from turning too far.

In tall grass, set up with more weight on the left leg.

Start the downswing with a shift of your hips to the left.

With your 3 wood, sweep the ball off the turf.

———————————————————

With a tight lie, think about a low finish.

———————————————————

Take the club back with your body, not your hands.

———————————————————

Turn your shoulders as far as possible.

———————————————————

Keep your weight on the inside of your right foot on the backswing.

———————————————————

Feel slight tension in your left shoulder at the top of the backswing.

The 'V's of your thumb and first finger should point to your right shoulder.

Fire your hips for power.

When setting up for the driver, tilt your spine away from the target.

The left side of your body should initiate the downswing.

Set up for a 3 wood with the ball two inches inside of the left heel.

In tall grass, use a steep angle to hit down on the ball.

With irons, squeeze the ball down against the grass.

Do not straighten your right leg on the backswing.

Keep the club head traveling down the target line as long as possible with the 3 wood.

In heavy rough, hinge your wrists early.

Make a downward strike with the hybrid club.

For a fade, move the ball slightly forward.

Get your shoulders turned and weight shifted.

With the driver, hit the ball on the upswing.

Shorten your backswing in the wind.

On the takeaway, feel your weight move to your right heel.

With irons, your weight should be distributed equally over the middle of your feet.

Do not grip the club too tightly.

Your hips should shift laterally at first, then start to rotate.

To hit a higher shot widen your stance and put the ball forward.

Swing down the slope with a downhill lie.

Begin the downswing by pushing down on your left foot.

Aim the face of the club before setting your feet.

Finish with your belt buckle facing the target.

Ignore the club striking the ball and just visualize a good swing.

When hitting down wind, use a full swing.

Increase your wrist hinge on your backswing for more power.

Turn completely on the backswing.

Aim for contact with the ball on the inside quarter of the ball.

For a draw, position the ball slightly back in your stance.

Lead with your hands on iron shots.

On a knockdown shot, do not re-hinge your wrists after impact.

Use one more club when hitting from a divot.

Take one more club on an uphill lie.

Make sure your posture is correct before every shot.

Don't hunch over with your back.

After shifting the hips left to start the downswing, unwind your hips.

With iron shots, focus on the front half of the ball.

Keep your hands relaxed at address.

Keep your right elbow in when hitting a drive.

A light grip allows you to release the club head through the ball.

Pinch the ball against the ground
with a tight lie.

The insides of your feet should be as
wide as the outsides of your
shoulders.

Don't even think about straightening
your right leg on the backswing.

Keep your wrist angle when you hit
in tall grass.

Keep your butt out on the set-up.

Hit the low stinger with a 3 iron or
with the driver.

Do not slide to the right on the backswing.

Tuck your left shoulder under your chin on the backswing.

Try to touch your forearms together as you swing through.

On the backswing, try to put your hands as far away from your head as you can.

On long irons, use a flatter swing, not a steep backswing.

Keep your spine angle the same as you swing back and through.

For more control, grip down.

Pay attention to tempo on all shots.

As you swing, rotate your left thigh
and turn the hips through.

Relax your shoulders.

Swing every club with the same
rhythm.

For a draw, use a stronger grip,
turning your left hand clockwise.

For more spin, use an open stance and open up the clubface.

———————————————

Make sure that your head is behind the ball at impact.

———————————————

Always aim for an intermediate target.

———————————————

Don't lift the club too sharply on your backswing.

———————————————

Hinge your wrists after the club reaches your hips.

———————————————

For a fade, open the clubface slightly.

———————————————

Ramblings: Number 6 Mistake— Chipping with Your Wrists

Ahhh, those pesky wrists! They are troublesome aren't they? They always want to get into the act.

If you are a superb athlete with exceptional hand eye coordination, then fine, chip with your wrists. Fuzzy Zoeller is a good example. He has wonderful touch and magic wrists. But we are not all Fuzzy.

The best way to consistently hit good chips is to simply rock your shoulders and arms together and keep your wrists quiet.

On a side hill lie, with the ball below
your feet, swing more vertically.

Don't place your hands too far away
from your body at set-up.

First shift your weight to your left
leg, and then turn your hips.

Don't cast the club, i.e., don't release
your wrists too early at the top.

Follow through with your arms and
hands toward the target.

Fire your hips through impact.

Tee the ball up lower for a low stinger shot.

Make a slow, smooth takeaway with the driver.

Bend from your hips; don't slouch over.

Use more club than you think for almost every shot.

Keep the club just short of parallel at the top of the backswing.

Put your weight on the inside of your right leg on the backswing.

Watch the ball closely as you hit it.

Make sure your shoulders are aligned with the target line at set-up.

Keep consistent speed on every shot.

For more power, delay turning your shoulders until your hips are unwinding.

For a knockdown shot, choke down on the club and take a shorter backswing.

Release the club after impact.

Hold the club in your fingers, not in the palm.

Once your shoulders stop turning back, your arms should too.

Don't grip the club too tightly.

Waggle the club to stay loose.

Don't swing too fast.

Use your rotation to raise the club, don't lift it up.

As you swing, think about driving your right knee into the ball.

Have a specific target in mind for each shot; don't just hit it down the middle.

Do not straighten your right leg on the backswing.

For a draw, close the clubface slightly.

When punching out, grip more tightly with your left hand.

Relax your hands at the top.

Think about keeping the same swing plane throughout your swing.

With the driver, take the club away in a wide arc.

Never try to swing too fast.

Stay in balance throughout your swing.

Use the same routine to set up for every shot.

On narrow fairways, hit a low stinger.

Don't look up as soon as you hit the ball.

Let the club do the work.

Play the ball in the middle of your stance for a low stinger.

Keep your arms and torso connected as you take the club away.

Concentrate on making solid contact with the ball.

Trust your swing.

Follow through low, through the ball; do not lift up.

Coil first with your shoulders and then turn your hips.

Let your wrists cock naturally; don't force them.

Swing the club with no tension.

The best swing path is slightly inside out.

Keep your hands high on the backswing.

Take the club away slowly and smoothly.

Don't muscle the shot; just let it unwind.

Avoid any kind of swaying during the shot.

Make sure the ball is not too far forward or too far back at set-up.

For irons, hit down on the ball; don't try to scoop under it.

Do not uncoil your shoulders too quickly.

The right arm should be higher than the left when the club is half way back.

Make sure the club is square at impact.

Make a full turn on every shot.

Keep your hands ahead of the club head at impact.

On the downswing, try to keep a 90-degree angle with your arms as long as you can.

Initiate the backswing by turning your shoulders.

Hit most shots with only 80% power.

Keep your chin up for good posture.

The arms should flow straight forward to the target.

Swing through the ball, not at the ball.

Keep light pressure with your grip.

Don't flip your wrists.

After impact, extend the club down the target line.

Use a steeper swing angle in the rough.

Tempo is the most important part of the swing.

Make sure to rotate around your spine.

Follow through on every shot.

Remember that it is a swing, not a hit.

Do not rush on the downswing.

Let the hands cross over after impact.

Commit to the shot.

Take the club back nice and slow.

Don't try to scoop the ball with short irons.

Keep your back straight and let your arms hang down naturally.

Shift your weight to the right leg on the backswing.

Take one practice swing to monitor your tempo.

Concentrate on having the right position at the top.

Roll your left hand over after impact.

Don't hunch over with your back.

Use the same pre-shot routine every time.

Keep your arms and body in synch.

Drop your hands to start your downswing.

On a downhill lie, set your feet farther apart.

Keep your head and chin up.

Never rush at the top.

Point your right elbow at your right hip on the downswing.

Maintain your wrist hinge as you start down.

Keep your left heel on the ground during the backswing.

On the takeaway the club head should be out in front of the body.

Keep your right elbow close to your right side on the downswing.

On side hill lies, choke down on the club.

In downhill rough, make sure your hands are ahead of the ball.

Keep the club head on plane.

Ramblings: Number 7 Mistake— Chipping with a Long Backswing

I don't know why people take such long backswings when chipping, but it is very common. This is not a good way to chip. A long backswing encourages deceleration which is always bad.

You should accelerate on all chips. Take a short backswing and accelerate a little bit with a long follow-through. Nothing but good stuff happens when you do this.

Drop into the 'slot' on the downswing.

Your spine should tilt away from the ball at address.

The right leg should turn forward through impact.

Turn your left foot out about 15 degrees.

Swing smoother with the driver.

Point the club parallel to the target at the top.

Come through with your right hip as you hit.

Pause very slightly at the top.

Do not slide your lower body forward during the shot.

Keep your left elbow close to your chest.

At impact your hands should lead the club head.

For a draw, toe the club in and swing along your stance line.

In a fairway bunker, play the ball
slightly back in your stance.

In wind, stand back farther from the ball
so you can swing around more.

Have only one swing thought per swing.
(You've got to be kidding!)

Always make a complete backswing.

Start your downswing slowly.

When hitting a wedge from the rough,
keep the clubface firm through impact.

For more spin, play the ball farther
back in your stance.

When between clubs, swing softer
with the longer club.

Keep your right wrist cocked as long
as possible.

Your left shoulder should be higher
than your right at address.

From hard pack, keep your lower
body quiet.

For power, coil against your flexed
right knee.

On an upslope shot, keep your shoulders parallel to the slope.

Don't separate your arms from your body.

Tuck your shoulder under your chin on the backswing.

Push off your right foot for more power.

Stay down as you hit through the shot.

Turn your chest through impact.

Maintain rhythm in your downswing.

As you follow through, your right shoulder should point at the target.

Take one more club when playing in the rain.

Turn your chest and arms through together.

Relax your shoulders and arms.

Align your feet, hips and shoulders parallel to the target.

Keep some bend in your right knee as you swing back.

Swing wide on the backswing with your driver.

Make sure you are balanced and centered at set-up.

Turn your left shoulder behind the ball.

Start your downswing with your hips.

In rough, play the ball back in your stance slightly.

Make sure your knees are flexed at set-up.

Keep your arms connected to your chest.

Maintain the triangle of your arms and shoulders throughout the swing.

Do not take any sand before you hit the ball in a fairway bunker.

Release the club head down the target line.

Do not ever reverse pivot.

Keep a firm grip when hitting from long rough.

Use timing, not effort, to get power.

Turn your left armpit as far as you can.

As you swing down, keep your hands low and the club head high.

Pick a specific target for every shot.

Rotate your right forearm through impact.

The first move on your downswing
should not be hurried.

Don't over-control the club.

For power keep your right elbow in
front of your hip as you swing.

Pause briefly at the top of your swing.

Proper tempo will solve a lot of
problems.

Put more weight on your left side when
hitting from a fairway bunker.

Don't drag the club through.

Keep your hands low at impact.

Feel confident as you stand over the ball.

With a downhill lie, align your shoulders with the slope.

As you follow through, touch the back of your left knee with your right knee.

Focus on solid contact with the driver.

Your arms and chest should move away together.

Maintain a consistent spine angle through the shot.

In downhill rough, use your most lofted wedge.

Rotate your forearms as you release the club.

Swing the club fluidly.

At the top of the backswing, point the shaft at the target.

For higher ball flight, put the ball more forward in your stance.

When hitting into the wind, use one more club and make a three-quarter finish.

Don't turn your shoulders too soon on the downswing.

With a downhill lie, flex your knees.

Don't pull the club back too far inside.

Your weight should be on the balls of your feet.

In fairway bunker, concentrate on hitting the ball first.

Open the clubface in tall grass.

For a draw, let your hands release after impact.

Take more club and swing within yourself.

Your left arm should fold after impact.

Turn your right hip and shoulder all the way through.

Set up with your head slightly behind the ball.

The divot should start just past where the ball was sitting.

Keep your weight on the inside of your right foot as you swing back.

Your shoulders should be behind the ball at the top of your swing.

Your right hip should turn through as you swing.

With the driver, don't hit down on the ball; sweep it.

Hit down on the ball with irons.

To cure a slice, close your shoulders more.

Don't break your wrists before impact.

Think "slow from the top."

Don't come up too soon after impact.

Feel a little tension in your left shoulder at the top.

Come through with your right arm,
right shoulder and right hip.

Finish toward the target.

Try to get your power from your hips
not from your arms.

Set up with your heels as far apart as
your shoulders.

Lean to the right a little at set-up.

Relax at set-up....relax.

Keep your eyes level with the ground.

Hit through the ball.

Don't be too mechanical.

Stick your butt out a little.

Take a slightly wider stance when
hitting in the wind.

Start the swing slowly and then
accelerate.

As you swing down, point the butt of
the club at the ball.

Your hip turn should be about half that of your shoulders.

Allow the hands to release after impact.

At address, turn your left foot out a little.

Hit the ball first and then the ground with irons.

Make a full turn with your back facing the target.

Get your right side through as you swing forward.

Finish with your chest facing the target.

Let your arms just drop with gravity.

Sweep the ball off the ground with a fairway wood.

In deep rough, swing down more steeply at the ball.

Stay balanced before, during and after your swing.

Keep your right elbow close to your right side on the downswing.

Ramblings: Number 8 Mistake— Coiling and Uncoiling

The best way to make a golf swing is to simply uncoil. This assumes that that you are coiled in the first place. Very few amateurs actually coil when they take the club back. It is not difficult, but it is also not very natural.

The secret to coiling is to keep the right knee bent with most of your weight on your right leg. Then turn your hips as far as you can. This is coiling. Of course, you take the club back with your chest and arms, but the coil is in your legs. That is where your power is.

There is a tendency to want to straighten the right leg, but avoid this at all costs. If the right leg straightens, you can turn your hips farther around, but this is not what you want to do. The idea is not to turn your hips as far as possible; rather, the idea is to keep your right knee bent and turn your hips so that you are fully coiled. This is where your power comes from.

Once you're nicely coiled, your first move for the downswing is to bump your left hip slightly towards the target. As you begin to uncoil, it is important to keep your right shoulder back. In other words, uncoil from the ground up, not from the shoulders down. The hips begin to uncoil and then the shoulders uncoil.

If you do it right, it is truly wonderful and easy. The only caveat is that the uncoiling action is not particularly natural. I can't think of any other sports in which we uncoil our hips in such a way, perhaps baseball. So stick with it. Practice at home without a club. Once you get this move down you will be a very happy golfer.

Pretend that you are confident before every shot.

With the ball below your feet, bend more with your knees, not your back.

Try to keep a fluid tempo.

Don't slide to the right as you swing back.

Extend your right arm after impact.

With an uphill lie, set up with your shoulders parallel to the slope.

Choke down for shots in deep rough.

Your shoulders and arms should work together.

Do not slide the hips.

Turn your left shoulder over your right hip.

Have a nice, consistent rhythm to your swing.

Make a meaningful practice swing.

At the top, do not dip past parallel.

Grip the club lightly.

Widen your stance to hit a low shot
into the wind.

Follow through completely on every
shot.

Keep your spine angle constant in
order to stay on plane.

Swing at only 80% of your strength.

Fire through with the right side.

Loosen your grip.

Don't sway when taking the club back.

Keep your wrists cocked as you come into the ball.

Keep your shoulders level on the takeaway, not dipped.

Come into the ball from the inside.

Turn your chest through impact.

The driver shaft should lean back at address.

Choke down on the club for
in-between yardage shots.

Visualize the face of the iron going
through the ball and toward the target.

Never flick at the ball with your wrists.

Set your hands forward on all irons.

Grip down for a punch shot.

Coil by moving your right buttock
back away from the ball.

Make a descending blow with your irons.

With a downhill lie, chase the ball down the hill with the club head.

Rotate around your spine on all shots.

With fairway woods, extend your arms down the target line.

Use a slower and smoother swing with long irons.

Commit to the shot.

Keep your back straight and bend
from the hips.

Begin the downswing slowly.

Keep your chin up; it will keep your
spine straight.

On a flop shot, keep your wrists
cocked as long as possible.

Trust your swing on every shot.

Try taking a shorter backswing with
the driver for accuracy.

On the backswing, keep your hands
as far from your head as possible.

At impact, your hips should be more
open than your shoulders.

Keep your weight on the inside of your
right foot on the backswing.

Lay up to your preferred distance,
say 100 yards.

Tee the ball up a little higher on your
drives.

For more control with the driver,
choke down an inch or two.

With a downhill lie, place the ball back in your stance.

On a downhill lie, try to swing very smoothly.

Hit down on the ball with a fairway wood.

Swing easier for more control with your driver.

Choke down on your short irons for greater control.

Start your swing by dropping, not turning, your right shoulder slightly.

Make sure to keep your head still
when hitting wedges.

Over-swinging reduces your
accuracy.

Accelerate through the ball on all shots.

Do not be tentative; commit to your
swing.

Stick your butt out as you take the
club back to the top.

Start your swing by bumping your
hips slightly to the left.

Then rotate your right hip towards the target.

At contact, the back of your left hand should be just ahead of the ball.

Take the club back with your shoulders and arms as one unit.

At set-up, let your hands hang down naturally, then grip the club.

Pause briefly at the top.

Start down slowly and then accelerate.

On the takeaway, keep your left arm
in close to your chest.

As your turn back, keep your right
knee bent.

Open your mouth a little to reduce
tension.

With irons, drive your right shoulder
down and through the ball.

Grip the club in your fingers, not in
your palm.

The angle of your bent right knee should
stay the same throughout the swing.

Close the clubface a little in order to hit a draw.

As you swing, drive your right shoulder down and through.

Finish with your right shoulder over your left foot.

Swing smoothly when the ball is below your feet.

Hit through the ball when using the driver.

Move your arms and shoulders as one unit as you swing down.

Delay the release of the club head.

Do not stand up as you take the club back.

To get spin, trap the ball against the ground.

Take the club back with your body, not your hands.

Keep the lag in the club as long as you can.

When your body stops turning back, don't continue moving your arms.

On the takeaway, keep your hands as far from your right ear as possible.

Do not let the club unhinge on the way down.

Visualize yourself making a perfect swing.

Take one more club and swing easily with every iron.

Your weight should move off your front leg on the backswing.

Keep your right palm facing down
through impact.

_____

Accelerate through and then release
the club.

_____

To start the downswing, the hips should
move before the shoulders.

_____

Swing your hybrid club just like a 7
iron.

_____

In the wind, take two clubs more and
grip down.

_____

In a fairway bunker, think about
sweeping the ball.

_____

Don't stop your shoulder turn too early.

Finish your swing in balance.

Never be afraid when hitting a golf shot; golf is *fun*.

If between clubs, simply choke down on the longer iron.

Always plant your feet solidly.

Turn your hips level; don't tilt them.

Relax at set-up; let your tension go.

Smack the ball with your right wrist at impact.

Rotate your forearms as you hit through the ball.

Make a flatter approach with your 3 wood.

Keep your spine angle the same throughout the shot.

Finish hitting the ball before you look up.

Make a relaxed swing with short irons.

Ramblings: Number 9 Mistake— Helping the Ball into the Air

Trying to help the ball into the air is especially problematic when there is something in front of you that you do not like, perhaps a lake or a pond. I was playing with a woman once who actually had a nice swing. When we played the hole with a water hazard up ahead, she proceeded to hit four balls into the water with her fairway wood. The idea is to hit *down* on the ball and then the ball will go *up*. This, of course, is counterintuitive. You have to trust the club.

The same is true for chipping. I played with another friend who hit chips that were low line drives—barely above the ground. He immediately blurts out: "I didn't get under it." No! You should never try to get the club *under* the ball with a chip. You hit *down* on the ball with the club and then the ball goes *up.* That's why the face of the club is slanted—it makes the ball go up! This takes some practice and you must learn to trust the club.

When setting up with the driver, your right shoulder should be lower than the left.

For a drive, your hands should be set up in front of your left thigh.

Bend from your hips, not your back. Don't try to steer the club.

The club should swoosh just passed the ball.

Play the ball back in your stance when hitting the driver off the deck.

Make a slightly descending blow
when hitting your irons.

For a lower ball flight, extend your
arms down the line.

Always accelerate through impact.

Make a balanced and athletic stance
when setting up.

Take only a three-quarter swing when
hitting a ball from the rough.

The first downswing move should be
lateral, without turning.

Keep your left arm relaxed and fairly straight on the backswing.

Your left wrist should face the target at impact.

To hit a higher shot, position the ball more forward in your stance.

Make a steeper swing than normal when hitting from the rough.

Keep your right elbow in on the downswing.

Take one more club when hitting from the rough.

Make a nice smooth swing when playing in the wind.

———————————

Stick your butt out on all shots.

———————————

Don't let your weight go outside your right foot during the backswing.

———————————

Keep your chin up to maintain the proper spine angle.

———————————

With an uphill lie, choke down and take one more club.

———————————

With a downhill lie, aim more to the left.

———————————

For a fade, play the ball slightly forward.

For a draw, play the ball slightly back in your stance.

Swing slower and smoothly when in the wind.

Tee the ball lower for more control with your driver.

Let your body turn through as you swing.

Swing smoothly and easily from fairway sand.

For more control, take the club back only three-fourths of a full swing.

Turn back with your shoulders; don't lift with your arms.

Don't bend over too much at address.

Put more weight on your left leg when hitting from the rough.

Take the club back slowly; there is no rush.

With irons, take a divot after hitting the ball.

Don't break your wrists too early on
the downswing.

You should release the club with your
turn, not with your hands.

Make a full turn back with your
shoulders.

Don't flip the club head at the ball.

Think about compressing the ball
when you make contact.

Your belt buckle should face the
target at impact.

Set up for a hybrid shot with the ball inside your left heel.

Keep your knees bent and relaxed on important shots.

Swing down slowly from the top.

Choke down for more control on all clubs.

Keep your feet and legs quiet.

Don't take the driver back past parallel.

Drop your right elbow into your side
on the downswing.

Maintain your posture as you begin
your backswing.

Move the ball farther back in your stance
for the higher lofted clubs.

Don't strangle the club; keep a nice
light grip.

Take the club back by simply turning
your shoulders.

Take one more club and swing
smoothly and easily.

Slow from the top is a good way to start your tempo.

Make sure your feet are far enough apart, especially with the longer clubs.

The downswing should begin with the hips, not the arms.

The ball will go farther with good timing than with muscles.

Watch the ball closely as you make contact.

Your hands should be relaxed at impact.

For better accuracy, try taking your driver back only halfway.

Keep your left arm in against your chest as you turn back.

Many swing problems can be cured with a correct stance at set-up.

Stick your butt out to maintain your spine angle.

Never swing at 100% power; stay within yourself.

To hit a higher shot, open the clubface
and open your stance.

———————————————————

Relax and enjoy the game. Nobody
really cares where your golf ball goes.

———————————————————

Practicing

Never hit more than three shots in a row with the same club at the range.

Practice hitting shots from bad lies and from divots.

Hit 20 putts from 3 or 4 feet from all four sides of the hole.

Hit ten lag putts from 20 to 25 feet.

Practice swinging with your feet together to develop the right release.

Learn the distance for each wedge swinging back only to the 9 o'clock position.

Aim for a specific target with every practice shot.

Speed is more important than line on putts; practice speed for distance control.

Make up putting games to keep practice interesting.

If your concentration is diminishing, stop practicing.

Practice long lag putts; they are the most important.

Try the cross-handed grip for a change when putting.

Swing from 9 o'clock back to 3 o'clock forward to learn the basic swing.

Practice hitting your driver with a half swing to keep arms and body in synch.

Practice hitting 15-foot to 20-foot putts so that they all go past the hole by 2 feet.

After a round, practice hitting the shots that were the most troublesome.

Chip with a sand wedge from all around the green.

Practice putts from the 12 points of a clock around a hole.

Practice using a one-handed swing with your right arm.

Practice your putts and chips every time you go to the range.

Before starting a round, practice playing the first three holes at the driving range.

Swing at 50% speed when learning a new swing idea.

Pull your right foot back to practice swinging with a good release.

Practice hitting your 5 iron the same distance as your 7 iron.

Always make a full finish with every practice swing.

Make one-handed swings to find your rhythm.

Practice chipping with a hybrid club and use a putting stroke.

Practice hitting from sand with your 9 iron to get more distance.

Practice pitches with 8 o'clock, 9 o'clock, and 10 o'clock backswings.

Practice 3-foot and 4-foot putts extensively.

Check your set-up posture in front of a mirror.

Practice your swing in super slow motion.

Swing with your right arm only to practice the correct weight shift.

Take one or two practice swings before every shot you hit on the range.

Take notes on what you learned at the range.

Practice hitting your driver a variety of distances with a full swing.

Ramblings: Number 10 Mistake— Not Having Enough Fun

It was a beautiful sunny Sunday in Seattle and I was driving across the floating bridge to go golfing with friends. I had played golf the day before and shot an excellent score, well, at least excellent for me. I had a great day and I was very pleased. But what if I did not play as well today? What if I double bogeyed the first two holes? Then my score would be lousy. I would be ruined for the day.

This really started to bother me and I was becoming quite trepidatious. What could I do? I drove on, puzzled and a bit worried. I realized that some shots will be good, many will be mediocre, a handful will be really lousy and a few will be spectacular. That is golf, right? And the score will be what the score will be.

The sun was out; the convertible top was down and I was contemplating this infernal game. I realized that I should just try my hardest on each shot and that was all I could do. Focus on trying to hit each shot the best I could. I certainly cared about the result but I could not *control* the result. All I could control was how I hit the ball.

So, that was my plan. I focused simply on hitting the golf ball. Guess what? I actually hit the ball pretty well. Not as good as the previous day, but better than normal. But more importantly, I had fun. I enjoyed being with my friends. I enjoyed being outside on a nice day.

No one cared what my golf score was...not my wife, not my kids, not my mother and not my friends. OK, I suppose I did care a bit, but I learned a good lesson. All I can do is hit the ball so I should just concentrate on hitting the ball. And the cool thing about golf...the ball always goes exactly where I hit it!

We golfers need to have more fun. No one cares what your score is. Golf is an extremely difficult game. And you are not that good! So, no more whining, no more bitching and no bad attitude.

Figure out a way to have fun on the course.

Funny story, and true: One of my friends plays golf only when she goes to Lake Tahoe. She is a terrible golfer. If she played 18 holes she would probably shoot 140. She only plays nine, however. We were playing one day and as we walked off the first green her husband was writing down the score. "I got a 16," she said. "I'll put you down for a 9," he replied. "No, I had a 16. I want to keep track and see how good I do. I want to see if I can beat my score from last week." Wow, I thought, unbelievable! But she was having fun and her goals were relative only to herself.

We did have a very enjoyable round of golf. Afterwards, we walked to the clubhouse with smiles and good attitudes. When is the last time you did that after shooting a 16 on one hole?